EASTERN MAGIC

Beautiful Designs of the Orient
to Color

BARRON'S

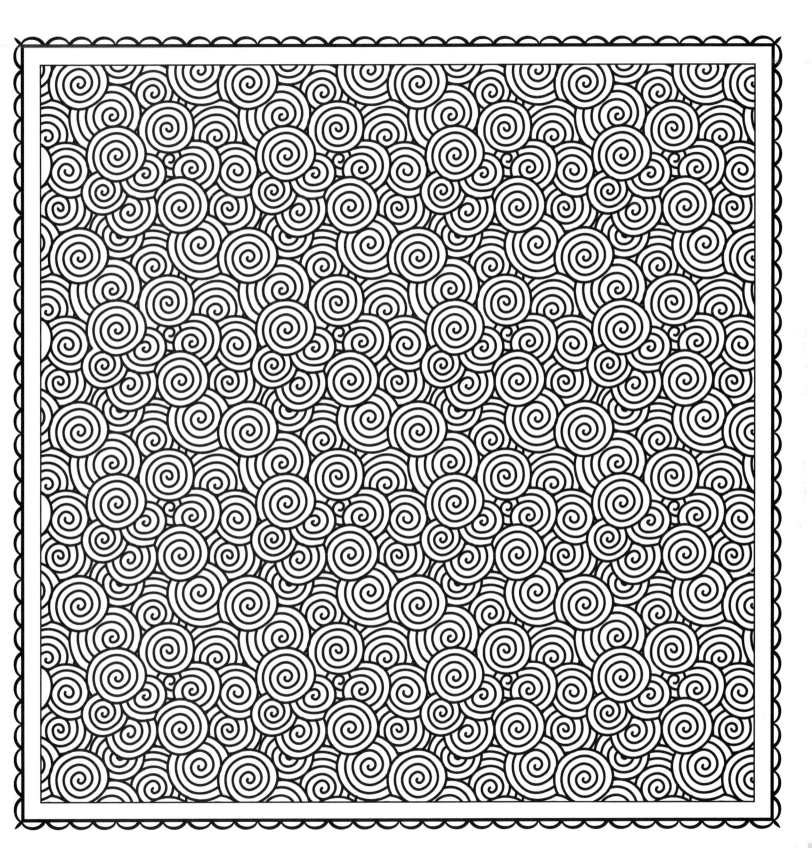

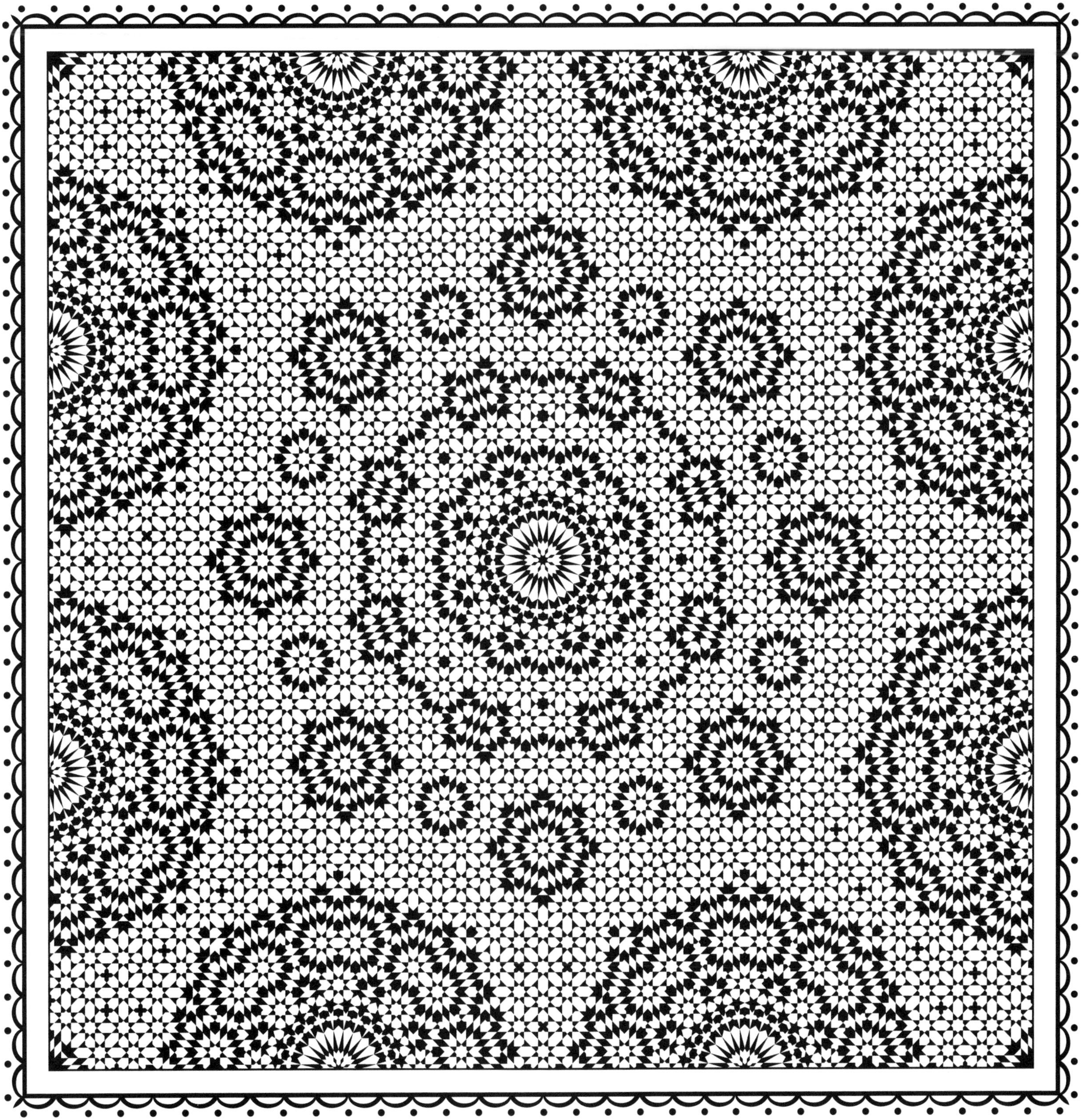

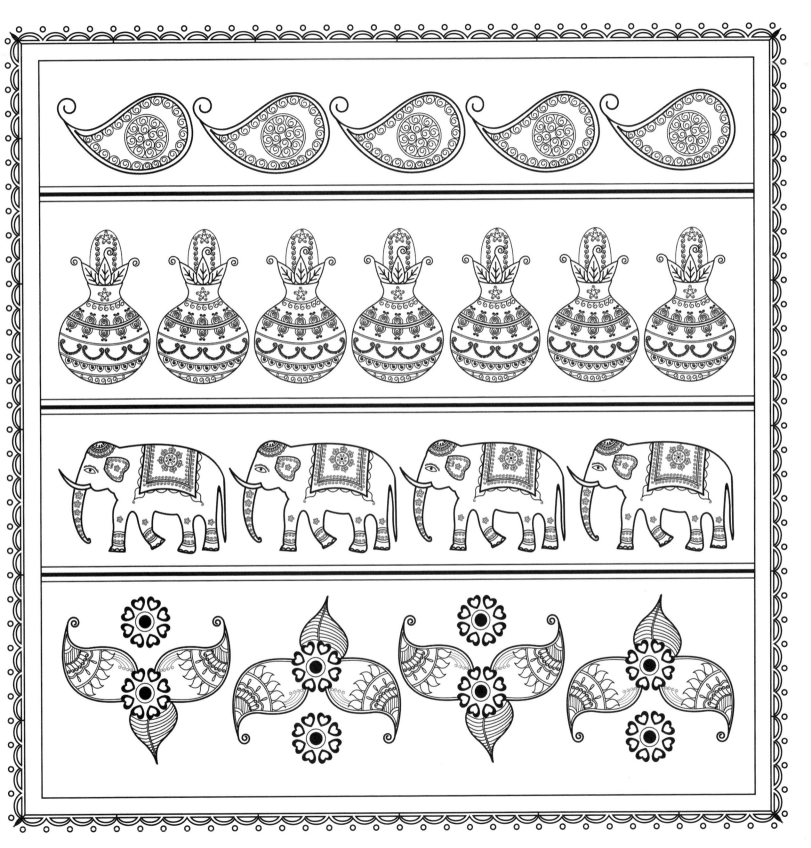

First edition for the United States, its territories
and dependencies, and Canada published in 2015
by Barron's Educational Series, Inc.

Original German title: *Orientalischer Zauber*
© Copyright 2015 arsEdition GmbH, München

All inquiries should be addressed to:
Barron's Educational Series, Inc.
250 Wireless Boulevard
Hauppauge, New York 11788
www.barronseduc.com

ISBN: 978-1-4380-0732-8

Cover Design: Grafisches Atelier, arsEdition
Interior Design: Eva Schindler, Atelier für grafische Gestaltung
Illustrations: Getty Images / Thinkstock
Colorization: Lea Schindler, Luisa Amann

Printed in the United States of America
9 8

For best results, colored pencils are recommended.